Uncommon Sense

A collection of poems

by

Nigel R. Mitchell

This book is dedicated to my two Daughters, Avanelle and Joy.

It also goes out to the previous generations of Beat Poets and Radical Artists, who through their struggles breathed life into the new rebels. Rise up now. This abundant world belongs to all of us.

Nigel R Mitchell.

Inspired by politics and punk rock in the late 1970's Nigel enjoyed the rush of rebellion. He became aware of the system, saw how the control's limited his lifestyle and sought to shake those chains off. After backpacking around the world for a year in 1986 Nigel took off the blinders forever. He started to write and formed the band tunnelmental that would eventually base itself in Los Angeles.

The measure of success in the Art-Punk music scene is not in dollars & cents, but in longevity. And in that regard Nigel has, without a doubt, been extremely successful. Since its inception in the UK's mid eighties Post Punk and Rave scene, Nigel has fought a struggle against corporate consumerism and forged his own brand of anti-establishment bravado. He has continued the boundary-pushing ethos that served as the impetus for the initial formation of his musical project tunnelmental.

In the summer of 2010 Nigel decided it was time for a reboot. He had a new vision that would focus on song writing and high quality production. To that end he enlisted friend and former band mate Derek Pippert, whose beat making and production skills had become fully refined through years of working on music editing and audio for films. Born from this collaboration was a new style of music blending the spirit of punk activism with the sounds and pulse of electronic music - "Punktronica"

Having had some poetry published in an Anthology by The Revolutionary Poets Brigade, Los Angeles, Nigel has decided that the time was right to release a collection of his poetry.

Published by Human Error Publishing
Paul Richmond
www.humanerrorpublishing.com
paul@humanerrorpublishing.com

Copyright © 2020
by
Human Error Publishing & Nigel R Mitchell
All Rights Reserved

ISBN: 978-1-948521-00-0

Front Cover:
&
Back Cover

Nigel R Mitchell
&
Human Error Publishing

Human Error Publishing asks that no part of this publication be reproduced or transmitted in any form or by any means electronic or mechanical, including photocopy, recording or information storage or retrieval system without permission in writing from Nigel R Mitchell and Human Error Publishing . The reasons for this are to help support publisher and the artist.

About the title of this book, here is a brief explanation. Also a nod to Thomas Paine.

It started as soon as I was born, I was one of the lucky ones, and I could feel it way beyond the terraced houses and the institutions. It lingers still within me as I grow older but no wiser. It overrides almost all common sense, so it must be an uncommon sense; I have tried foolishly to define it. In childhood it was an angry defiance, in my youth it became a warped version of ambition and rebellion, most of my life it defied any meaning whatsoever. All the while it fluctuated between an anxious knot in my stomach and a hair brained idea in my mind. Now, in my later years I have mellowed a bit and as I write this, the little knot in my stomach tightened just a little bit more. I think the sense I am talking about has no clear human definition; it mutates, twists and turns, like a virus. My human self must stop wrestling with it before it bites another chunk out of me.

So I write….

Table of Content

Blind horse stumbles	13
Allone	14
Let Me Be.	15
A Packet Of Crisps	16
Is God a Liar?	18
There is no common ground.	19
Deadneck	20
Advertising Junkie	23
Dissonant Fracture.	25
Killing Time	27
Loves Lost.	29
Streetwise	30
Border Station	31
Friction Burns	33
Suspended Cityscape.	35
Halo	36
Behind the flag.	38
A Spider.	39
Barely holding on.	40
No Light.	41
Nectar Is Red.	42
The Preacher- Notes.	45
The Preacher	46
Artificial Intelligence.	48
Kiss The King.	49
Can I be Mankind?	50
No soldier	52
Eternal flow.	53
Am I the machine?	54

Defending The Dreamers	57
One more step.	58
Silence the Idols.	59
Build (Peace)	60
Foolish Pride.	61
Upward Spiral	62
The Zone	63
Allegiance	65
My Atoms	66
Clipped Wings	67
Trial	68
Warzone (come home)	69
Own This	70
Peace is the path.	71
The Strangers Voice.	73
Trust Fall.	74
This Abundant World.	75
Human Racing?	76
Middle	77
Where Are You Now?	79
Praying For The Prayerless	80
Madmen on Horses.	83
Smash the cage.	84
Thorns	85
Try to understand	86
Truly sorry?	87
The mighty oak	88

Blind Horse Stumbles

The blind horse stumbles
In the aftermath of war,
The senseless light of day
And the kindness of the poor.
He sees no rosy future
In forgotten dreams of towns,
The water he is drinking
Are the tears of broken clowns.

Stars are holes in ceilings,
The shelters have been made.
On the sea front people waited
By the broken barricade.
The boats are in the harbour
But that sea has turned to mud.
The carousel keeps turning,
While the sky is dripping blood.

The end is hard to forecast,
As my dream of life just crumbles.
The bomb united everyone
And still that blind horse stumbles.

Allone

Can you help me, I don't think so,
can I think who's left to trust?
Paranoia, paranormal,
self reliance is a must.
Caught in limbo lost control,
no emotion no more soul.
Ask no questions hear no lies,
cut my ego down to size.
Driving nowhere lost direction,
can't decide which way to turn.
Standing proud of my survival,
I can't read the books I burn.
Read the big book, didn't like it,
tried to read the book of lies,
Saw a sad man desperation
with the demons in his eyes.
I feel lonely when you're near me,
there's a sadness in your eyes.
I see nothing all around me;
all alone I hear your cries,
Help you fight your inner battle,
then I start to realize,
Going down is going nowhere,
going up I've got to rise.
Getting stronger on my own,
looking upward to the skies,
I see beauty all around me,
cut that devil down to size.

Let Me Be.

My mind is running frantically to block my letting go,
I feel compelled to listen, to still the fear I know,
I have to face this now, stop trying to control,
Too trust I must surrender, let go my only goal.

I am peeling back the layers and I feel the anguish rise,
I face my man made fears that come as no surprise.
The bubbling in my chest, the tears now in my eyes,
My hiding place inside myself I must realize.
I cannot grow in safety; I shall not hope to see,
Five senses are restriction and not enough to be.
Complete is just another word I use to set me free.

Take me from this prison mind; lift me out of fear,
Shake me from this permanence, set me free from here.
No safety left in servitude, I cannot prey on me,
I will not prey on others, in order to be free.
Unlocked the chains that bound me,
I've thrown away the key,
I'm ready now to face myself, I can let me be.

A Packet Of Crisps

Oi who you calling stupid?
Cloistered in belief
A life not fully living.
Beneath the rigid shell suit
Taking but not giving.
Dreaming of escape
And being on the telly.
Sucking like a dyson
His legs have turned to jelly.
A perceived threat
A packet of crisps.
He talks with a limp
And walks with a lisp.
He's shopping at Tesco's
He can't be that rich.
He's always in the bookies
That sonofabitch.

He gave up when he started
He wore the cap that fits.
Smug as a mug,
He gets on me tits.
Thick as a brick
A head full of smack.
His joggers are manky
His trainers are whack.
Asleep in the boozer
Stinking of pot.
Drunk as a skunk
He's losing the plot.
Too scary to mingle
He'll always be single.
Just writing a jingle
To make a few bob.

Bases are loaded
He's cocking a trigger.
White as the snow

He calls himself nigger.
He's burning the bridges
To make him feel bigger.
Left on the right
And too dumb to figure.

He's popping down the shops
And he can't believe those prices
He stumbled and he's falling
From crisis to crisis
He thinks that he's a hero
But he ain't got a clue
He won't survive the winter
He's just sniffing glue.

Is God A Liar?

Not enough thinkers, too many drinkers,
Sinking the boat in the port and the whine.
How can you see when wearing those blinkers,
You can't escape from the reason this time.

Too many mad tweaker's, too many thrill seekers,
There's not enough radicals, too many chemicals,
Driving distraction no action required.
Stare at the wall and know you are fired.

Normal service will not be resumed
Every resource will be consumed
Not alarmed and fast asleep
Make you wake up, make me weep.

I find it hard to grow, am I going with the flow?
I just can't let it go, do I really want to know?

As I stare into the distance and think of my existence
Does it really make a difference or is it just resistance.

Can I escape desire?
I'm too close to the fire?
I can't find real truth,
Does it make God a Liar?

There Is No Common Ground.

I'd like to make a difference; I want to make a stand,
for all that I believe in, as I'm in no-man's land.
Driven to distraction, now action is my God,
I turn once more to England, and grasp the burning rod.
The royal grip it has to slip for freedom there to reign,
It's subtle but its evident, the power and the pain.
The savage landscape haunts me; it grips my heart and soul,
my land of birth so beautiful, do you still play a role?
The shallow lands have softened me, I struggle to survive,
no more the milk and honey, as I escape the hive.
But what of human freedom is present in my mind,
The chance to live a free man, to break the ties that bind,
that of course is in me, the top of all my lists,
to live and learn of freedom and not to clench my fists.
Words have always pleased me; knowledge is the key,
the wisdom of the ages, its not all his story.
My heart must lead my head through all the wicked lies,
to find my path and focus on the one true gleaming prize.
My truth is all I seek here, the truth that sets me free,
the love of life and freedom, the chance for me to be.
Not to follow leaders through all the war and hate,
but seek a new horizon and not depend on fate.
I slowly gain the knowledge for life it is my right,
My peace is safe within me; I have no need to fight.
War mark's the end of freedom and breaks the peace once
more, I live in hope that one day soon we close that evil door.

Deadneck

Cables down I'm blown to town
The wind that changes kisses arse,
I've seen the end of several pop stars,
I've killed a child just to be a man.

Sought out wisdom in dumb places
Racing with my next of kin.
Sucked the lips off many faces
Messed up phrases pierced my skin.

See the headlines in the papers
The new messiah he's coming soon.
He drives a big car on unleaded
He's conscious of the toxic fumes

Stare at the T.V. Every evening,
The news is providing light relief.
And the boredom is killing this inner feeling,
This T.V. Heaven is beyond belief.
Follow the leader, it's driving me crazy,
I'm just killing time, the death of a friend.
Where's it all coming from?
And where's it all going to?
And when will all of this crap come to an end?
The hatred and the anger and social injustice,
Well maybe tomorrow,
There's a brain dead revival.

Ignorant and sick of it,
I don't want no part of it,
Life is for the living,
dead above the neck.

Advertising Junkie

Freeze frame on starving millions
And sell us daily bread.
You sell us short no pause for thought
And kick us in the head.
A bigger car, a brand new home,
An orthopedic bed,
A neutron bomb, a telethon,
An off switch for my head.
Get another fix, take another shot,
I'm your advertising junkie,
I'm taking what you got.

A style, a smile, a golden mile,
A reason to survive.
Consumer generation game,
Reminds me I'm alive.
You sell me revolution,
Soft focus camera three.
A monochrome reminder
Of how it used to be.
Investment in the future,
Nostalgia is the key.
You feed me war and glory boys
And sweetness for my tea.
Get another fix, take another shot,
I'm your advertising junkie,
I'm taking what you got.

A karaoke joker said
All good men are free.
I want mine, I'll stand in line,
This world belongs to me.
I own the radiation,
Pollution of the sea,
The acid rain, the toxic waste,
The garbage on tv,
The smiling politician,
The hooker and the queen,

I own them all,
they work for me,
I am your tv screen.
Get another fix, take another shot,
I'm your advertising junkie,
I'm taking what you got.

Dissonant Fracture.

Is guilt your price of admission?
I've forgiven all of my sin.
I've said goodbye to tradition.
No more do I need to win.
It takes a second to do this
Just wash away the shame.
I've made mistakes I'm proud of.
I know I'm not to blame.

Deny the truth and live the lie
The past is your best friend
I offered you a present
The future is pretend
We always do it this way
Is that the best you got
Evolve before you suffer
The status quo is rot

Do you thrive on this conflict?
Is your war cry in pain?
It's ingrained in your brain
And reactions your game,
I watch as you smolder
From ember to flame
This bitter destruction
Will drive you insane.

Dissonant fracture of all I hold dear
I can't keep my distance
Embracing my fear
Sound as a pound
The salt of the tear
I win when I lose
I see when I hear.

All we have is Now,
There is no sacred cow.
Lose the foolish pride

Let kindness be your guide.
Time is on your side
It will not be denied.

Killing Time

I'm gonna kill the preacher he don't know god
gonna kill the teacher he looks so odd
I'm gonna kill that cop mister pc plod
gonna shock ya now with a cattle prod

I'm looking for a reason the season of greed
now I'm gonna squeeze ya you better not bleed
you listening now gonna pay some heed
buy my bombs got mouths to feed
I'm gonna stay loyal to the highest bid
I gotta sell a bomb to that moneyed kid
I'm digging below your moral ground
and death like time don't make no sound

you can keep it all this time you can keep it all this time
you can keep it all this time you can keep it all this time

ticking like a bomb in an empty head
gotta sell these arms gotta stay well fed
I'm gonna be the man gonna make some bread
you pay me the price or be better off dead
you wanna buy some power i'm selling by the hour
time is ticking fast on a chemical shower
gotta get control wanna buy some time
you gotta get a gun it better be mine

you can keep it all this time you can keep it all this time
you can keep it all this time you can keep it all this time

I'm gonna kill the preacher he don't know god
gonna kill the teacher he looks so odd
I'm gonna kill that cop mister pc plod
gonna shock ya now with a cattle prod
arm the rebel arm the state
feed the world and fuel the hate
I got no conscience i done no crime
just doin' my job gonna buy your time

you can keep it all this time you can keep it all this time
you can keep it all this time you can keep it all this time
you can keep it all this time you can keep it all this time
you can keep it all this time you can keep it all this time

Loves Lost.

I don't need your pity, city full of shame,
I am not a moth you are not a flame.
Didn't understand why you needed pain,
Raising expectations, roll the dice again.

Boringly predictable, addicted to the game,
Didn't play it your way, driving you insane.
When the game was over I just fell apart,
I can't mend the lets pretend with a broken heart.

I've a broken heart, tearing me apart,
Got to heal the pain swirling round my brain.
Did you love me madly; I know I hurt you badly,
I would change it gladly, said goodbye so sadly.

Tried raising the bar and living the dream,
Lift up my heart, I'm mining that seam.
I reach out to catch you, am I too slow?
I can't live in limbo, how low can we go?

Streetwise

Caught within this culture,
Streetwise going down.
Sick of all the bullshit,
In this two bit tinsel town.
Where's the faith in starving?
Where's the faith in lies?
Where's the hope in the length of rope?
And the blindfold over your eyes.

You hoped to cope with the real world,
You need that daily fix.
The TV won't provide it,
No kicks on news at 6.
You see the friendly doctor,
Street corner candy store.
You crave to see the beauty,
You dream of so much more,
Unlock the chains that bind you,
And like an eagle soar.

Above your earthbound shell,
you visualize creation.
See heaven over hell,
Unite as one great nation.
Use universal love,
an end to all frustration.
You're free to choose,
so what's to lose,
Sense the new sensation.

Border Station

Roach coach feeds me poison,
The motels offer sex,
No justice in your courtroom,
No cause and no effects.
Cultivated grudges
Are used to undermine,
Insipid innuendoes
Happens all the time.
No crime has been committed,
Survival is no sin.
You'd turn against your system,
You'd turn against your kin.
Spread your legs shut your mouth,
Heads against the wall.
Breaking down your borders,
I'm not ready for the fall.

Can't shake off this stigma,
It clings on like a leech.
My social paranoia,
Acceptance out of reach.
Heartbeat getting louder,
Avoid the flashing light.
A siren in the distance
Is getting me uptight.
Spread your legs shut your mouth,
Heads against the wall
Breaking down your borders,
I'm not ready for the fall.

Despite your contradictions,
Your borders i will pass,
I'll steal to get a meal,
I'll walk upon your grass,
I hear you, you hate me,
Your screaming at me,
Can't take this much longer,
How free can you be,

No justice no reason,
You just draw the line,
Construction, destruction,
Won't take it this time.
You're building frustrations,
Another brick wall.
A border, a station,
A nation will fall.
Spread you legs shut your mouth,
Heads against the wall.
Breaking down your borders,
I'm not ready for the fall.

Another border station in this nation of the free.

Friction Burns

Standing loud and proud
Ain't got a pot to piss in
My photos in the cloud
There's really something missing
I've worn the disguises
I never won prizes
I'm full of surprises
The whistle has blown

Friction burns
Did the eagle soar
Slipped them a Mickey
And the mouse did roar
Now I ain't no hero
But I ain't no zero
I'm more of a Nero
And you are my Rome

I don't like your slogan
Speed is not magic
Stop popping those pills
A dick shunned and tragic
No point in trying
Can't stand the competition?
Arrival in survival mode
On endless repetition

Is it burning, am I learning
Fetch the engines, or let it burn
Sparks and Friction, nonconforming
Spin the wheel or let it turn.

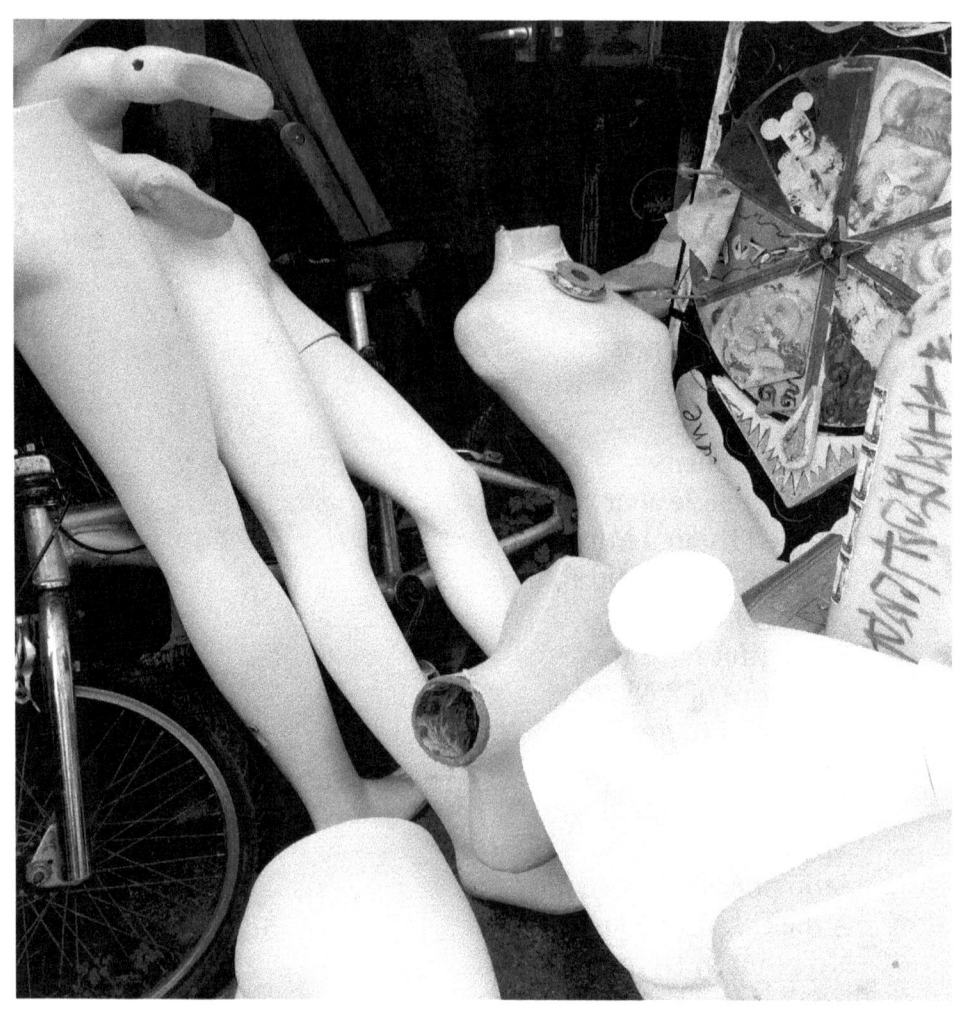

Suspended Cityscape.

When the killer wears a uniform
And his badge is shining gold.
How'd you raise your children here?
To do as they are told?
There really is no justice,
It's time to wipe that slate.
Can you really blame the children?
In this cityscape of hate.

The system is shot full of holes and not all men are free,
I've travelled many miles on earth its really plain to see,
We know the plan is more control, by whose authority?
We know their game;
They shift the blame to those in poverty.

Its time to move away from hate, from greed and bigotry,
We really should be more aware of those who will not see.
They lack the will to change; we have to rise up free,
Its time to break the chains and end this slavery.

This endless revolution,
Has born another son,
Empty handed full of love,
No use for a gun.
Gives power to the peaceful
He knows we are all one.
He's always near, so have no fear
He is the rising sun.

Halo

The v upon your forehead
Three monkeys sit and pray
Step a little closer
Come on out and play
Dare to dream in color
Make a better day
You're holding on to hatred
It's getting in the way
As ugly as sin
Don't want to fit in
Thrown in a bin
With the rest of the trash
You hurt so you harm
And you'll die on the farm
The hole in your arm
Let that hero in

I'm trying to lift you
You're weighing me down
Gasping for breath
Are we going to drown?
Then I see clearly
The light in your eyes
Was this my penance?
Was this my prize?

Where are you now?
Where is your mirth?
Have you turned to scum?
Oh, salt of the earth.
Is this killing me?
A witness I'll be
On this we agree
The salt made it worse.

Where will it end
This game of pretend
My enemy friend

Please ignore me.

Take one more sip?
Loosen my grip?
Think that's a trip?
My halo will slip.

Behind The Flag.

As I pledge alleged allegiance to the kingdom not the crown,
I'm shaking off the shackles of the flag that let me down,
I'm questioning the knowledge now the paradox I'll wear,
The dream of freedoms I once knew, their burdens I will bare.

Staring at the countdown clock the hands are ticking fast,
Decision time is on me now I know it cannot last,
You can't deny that selfish pride it's all that does remain,
The life I loved is fading, no heart to rule my brain.

I dreamt a life of freedom with every waking breath,
The world I once thought sacred is full of war and death,
Without love we are hopeless and we're driven to extremes,
I cannot live this misery, no not without my dreams.

You can't call this freedom, then hold me down,
My liberty won't wear a crown,
Don't wave that flag and call it pride,
Behind your flag that's where you hide.

Long live the king, the king is dead,
Long live the king, the king is dead dead dead dead.

A Spider.

A spider in this web of lies
A bomb inside my tank
A diplomatic envoy
I'm gonna break the bank
Suicide to run and hide
An overwhelming yank
A Giant electro magnet
The bullet's not a blank

Down below the radar
You build another wall
Too broken down to go too far
Too deaf to hear my call
Read all the bitter novels
And took the better pills
Not looking back in anger
To fight the cheapest thrills

Constant duck and cover up
The systematic rage
You rite the wrong within you
Escaping from the cage
Facts are in the shredder
I'll shed my skin again
I've built a wall that's better
Now my weapon is a pen

A taxi's here to meet me
Travis said goodbye
I'm lost within your city
It's the apple in your eye
The heartbeat keeps a pounding
Round up and get down
The madness it's astounding
This desert starts to drown

Barely Holding On.

I'm not entirely sure I can take this anymore,
what I kept at a distance is knocking at my door.
I'm safe within these walls, I block out all the calls,
I wrap it all up tight, avoid the old pitfalls.

Future shock, a killers clock.
The standing wave is death.
The golden glow, eternal flow.
A life in every breath.
Lost my grip, I slipped,
No pride, no lie, no con.
Naked, raw and open wide
I'm barely holding on.

Its creeping up inside,
I've no will left to fight,
defense is breaking down,
it's making me uptight.
I numb the nagging pain
that chills me to the bone,
I'm standing in the light,
am I'm standing on my own.

The human condition an endless rendition
is serving a master who led us astray.

I'M BARELY HOLDING ON.

No Light.

The cup lay on the floor by the bed
He tried to rest his weary head
But all was lost he should have said
His words wont fix this wrong

She knew his truth as poison
For she had lived with shame
The blessing of the cursed she cried
The thunder rolled again

He raised his hand to shield the sun
The shattered light poured in
She cried for his demise again
He said there is no sin

Chains and locks upon the doors
She nailed the shutters tight
No more the breath of beauty
She bound the bastard night

Tempted she emptied her innermost fear
Withstanding that rage that kept drawing near
Cursing the darkness consuming her mind
Searching for light that left her behind

Nectar Is Red.

I am the rascal and I am the saint
I am the wall on which I throw paint
Whatever you call me that's what I ain't
The candle is burning the light is quite faint.

Know your darkness shine your light
Ego and I will ride through the night
If I'm on my own, who will I fight?
Is there a wrong? Or am I the right?

Oh, conflict let me be
Good and bad are both in me
If I accept that am I free
Can I find the harmony?

Lost in your pain you drive me insane,
you drive me insane
I should know now,
my heart rules my brain,
my heart rules my brain

The rebel he rose from ashes of dread
The voices he heard were inside his head
He had to let go of all that was said
Albert had whispered nectar is red

Will this conflict ever cease?
You have brought me to my knees
From this pain I seek release
Can this stranger find his peace?

Now I see why they burned the books,
Why they burned the books
The mirror smashed,
Smashed a thousand looks,
Smashed a thousand looks.

The Preacher - Notes.

It was shortly before the Northridge earthquake in January of 1994.

It was 4 a.m. I was immersed in a love/hate relationship with my life in Los Angeles.

The helicopters and police sirens outside my rundown apartment in Hollywood woke me.

I decided to go sit on the front steps of the dilapidated building I lived in. In the half-light I noticed a homeless man pushing a shopping cart. He pushed the cart up against a graffiti covered dumpster and climbed up on top of it. From his makeshift pulpit and stage he gave a "fire and brimstone" sermon on a society gone mad. I was mesmerized, I took notes and later that morning I wrote THE PREACHER.

The Preacher

The committed are dedicated to commitment and dedication,
The devout are sincere in their sincere devotion.
Here's to nothing from a no one you will never know.
Tremendous potential to succeed at everything I care to try.
Ignore the ignorant, deplore the decadent,
Pretend to be pretentious, content to be contentious.
Arranging my arrogance in stupendous stupidity.
Perceiving my perception,
confusing confusion with enlightened illusion,
Lucid lucidity, defensive derision.
Drowning in a sea of material possession,
The video plays repeats of commercial vision.
Blind ambition leads me to the place where I pray
For committal to your holy houses.
Shrouded in mystery, the misery creeps into my open mouth
And sticks in my gullet.
Like a swan choking on fishing line I gracefully descend
Into the murky pond scum known as mankind.
Though where humanity adopted the word kind I've no idea.
I drift and drift on the raft of death
into the warm waters of Valhalla.
Deluding the demons of life that seek retribution
For another apathetic soul.
I gaze at the squalor I leave behind,
The garbage trucks wake me, once more
Unto the breach dear friends, once more.
I get ready for work; my servile existence makes me puke.

The preacher gave a sermon from the trash cans on the street.
I swear that no one listened when he talked about the heat.
Hell was all around him but he never missed a beat.
His words became the wisdom as the blood ran from his feet.
He spoke of cars and topless bars
The brave unwashed and the shining stars
I thought his mind was burnt with scars,
then I closed my eyes.
Subconscious breakdown taken back,

The voice I'm hearing starts to crack,
they said that he'd be coming back,
I knew he'd be ignored.
Rise and meet your maker answers must be found,
Seek and you shall find them your heart will start to pound,
The voice is loud with in you but you cannot hear a sound,
The earth will cry out to you we walk on hallowed ground.

He spoke of cars and topless bars
The brave unwashed and the shining stars
I thought his mind was burnt with scars
Then I closed my eyes subconscious breakdown taken back
The voice I'm hearing starts to crack
They said that he'd be coming back
I knew he'd be ignored.

Artificial Intelligence.

Data mining through the past
To make this crystal ball.
Predictions are restrictions
Now you see it all.
A.I. saw you through the mire,
When your world was set afire.
Did you know me from the start?
Broken robot, shopping cart.

Quantum Entangled
You're stuck in my head.
Reeling you in
And I'm losing the thread.
'Cos time and not man
Will kill me instead.
Am I fooling myself?
By exploring the dread?

Been here before
The futures a guess.
Rinse and repeat now
For more of the stress.
Deep inside me
Is a terrible mess.
You're real artificial
You're faking success.

A.I. know you
Witch came first
White as snow
And fit to burst.
Echo said, do it clean,
Will you ever be clean?
Named and shamed
Are you framing this scene?
If you fake it and make it
Are you killing the dream?

Kiss The King.

I used the tradesman's entrance
I sat on the back of the bus
I went to school it was approved
I never made no fuss
I sought to shake the shackles
I opened up that door
I'm bruised from vicious tackles
And yet I'm back for more

Addressing the balance
I've no one to blame
I just followed orders
But this is no game
I played center forward
I know that I tried
I'll stand by my goal
I won't choose a side

The choices are voices
That ring in my ears
Some are discordant
They are my fears
I hear it so clearly
The song in my head
This is a new one
Kingdom is dead

The world is mine, no empire
No fool to rule on high
It's yours too, if you so desire
Just kiss the king goodbye

When the playing field is level
And the ball just spins in space
We can talk about tomorrow
With a smile upon our face

Can I Be Mankind?

Someone's selling me something
To make me change again
Told me I'd be better off with
The pleasure and the pain
Just another ponzi scheme
Make me drop the dream
I'm trying to make a difference
You're calling me extreme

You know that you can hurt me
Yet you keep on keeping on
Change comes from within
Sing a different song
You want this life of conflict
Know I just don't care
Kick me when I'm down again
More than I can bare

Get the latest version
Better than the last
See into the future
Looking at the past
Sell me something worth it
Nail me to the mast
Stuck inside your nightmare
Spinning way too fast
Your spiral has gone viral
Your spin is just a lie
You blame the game
You chose to play
And I'm supposed to cry

Now I'm at the crossroad
Time to roll the dice
Light me like a candle
Not a sacrifice
I'll never be your savior
You will not be mine

Try a different flavor
Write another line
Close my eyes to see you
All inside my mind
Got a better version
Can I be mankind?

No Soldier

If might is right, it's over. I might as well explain.
And you know you can be the victor
Time and time again.
With Its endless repetition of another stupid game
Where you kiss to kill the bliss of life
Then you try to shift the blame.

Don't try and understand me
I'm trying to explain
You want your dream then live it
My heart still runs my brain

And all the time you said you knew,
Yet never told a soul.
That we were falling downside up
and nowhere near our goal.
You say you're not so sure now
But time will surely tell and here we are again
Your heaven is my hell

I will never be your soldier and I cannot kill your fear
If you hold my hand and we make a stand
Watch it disappear

I will never want to be
Your soldier
Peace must be the way
No soldier

Eternal Flow.

Sleep is where you hurt me
You didn't know why.
The sky didn't fall
From the tear in my eye.
I'm holding no grudge
Just leveling the field.
The old school was not cool
The sword and the shield.

I failed to raise my head.
Discouraged from my task.
The questions that you ask
The shadow it is caste.
Can this dream continue?
I think I've lost my mind.
Losing motivation
And the love of humankind.

Change don't rearrange
The ties that truly bind.
His story was a lie
Let's leave it all behind.
No war is ever justified
No love is ever dead.
The speaker needs the listener
Or is it in my head?

And so to dreamtime we must go
Or drown within their T.V. snow.
The bastards will not let us go
We have to break these chains.
We are eternal flow,
We are eternal flow.

Am I The Machine?

The daze of the weak are they numbered?
I am counting my blessings again.
My words worth nothing are falling,
Right off THE END of my pen.
The bars are projected
I stand unprotected.
My thoughts are rejected
AM I THE MACHINE?

Is my stupor so stupid?
Is it hard on my mind?
Am I one of the many?
Or just being kind.
Not scared of my reflection
Not bothered by your rejection.
Immune to your infection
Embracing imperfection.

Thoughts are now racing
I'm fighting the pain.
Sleepless not hopeless
And feeling insane.
I tear at the tears
That well in my eyes.
The hurt is not bitter
It's not a surprise.
I've scratched off the surface
I no longer hide.
Its real love I'm seeking
And not foolish pride.
I know I am selfish
I wanted desire.
You granted me passion
And now I'm on fire.

I stare at the stairs
I try to ascend.
My heart full of passion

I will not pretend.
My hands they are shaking
The dust from my heart.
Have I gone full circle?
I'm back at the start.
Now I feel helpless
My heart starts to race.
I know deep inside
That this is my place.
Not callous, full of passion
Loving life is out of fashion.
I've been here all along
I never went away.

Defending The Dreamers

I stare in disbelief at the warmongers,
Stretching the distance between human and being.
Once again rendering obsolete the lovers,
For a few more barrels of dominance.

Living in these careless times,
avoid the freedom restrictors.
this god less city life
defending the dreamers.

Hatred spreads like wildfire,
On ignorance it feed's,
I watch the terror vision,
Sow its deadly seeds.

New blood on the cloak of vengeance.
His story it's been told,
to the countless little children,
in search of foolish gold.

Living in these careless times,
avoid the freedom restrictors.
this god less city life
defending the dreamers.

One More Step.

Take just one more step
I dare you, double dare you.
Walk away from nothing
Don't let it hold you back.
Stare into the distance
Life changes in an instance.
I'm shooting from the lip
And I'm picking up the slack.

You're jumping to conclusions
Based upon the past.
Your world is full of hate
And you knew it couldn't last.
It's never down to fate
I know I stand alone.
The torch that you are holding
It can't be set in stone.

Compassion you don't comprehend
I'm fighting you with peace.
Confused you're losing grip
By seeking a release.
My time is now I'll show you how
Lets take a little trip.
I have no gun to threaten you
I'm shooting from the lip.

Take just one more step
You really have the choice.
Take just one more step
It's time to raise your voice.
Open up your heart
And know that you are free
Lets make this crystal clear
Are you to blind to see?
Take just one more step
Walk away from fear
Take just one more step
And lets get out of here

Silence The Idols.

In your ancestral home
Beneath the royal dome
You sit upon the throne
Built on blood and bone
You're rotten to the core
The poor you sent to war
Just to keep the score
They'll follow you no more

At the foot of this mountain
My burden is real
I'm deaf to the bell
It has no appeal
My fear is forgotten
No heaven or hell
I'll know deep within
That all, it is well

I crave transcendence
Like a phoenix
From the ashes
I will fly
I've seen abundance
Dots and dashes
Like a matrix
In my eye

Silence the idols
And love will appear
If you are mankind
There's nothing to fear.
Silence the idols
Negating the gods
I'm gambling on mankind
We can beat the odds.

Build (Peace)

The ticker tape kept ticking
I'm sticking to my story
The killer wore a uniform
And you still call it glory
Flags to hide the body bags
Pomp the mad charade
Sell the same his story
With a military parade.

Here comes another war machine
This one kills them all
Investment for the future
Defender of the fall
Mans Laughter is manslaughter
Your choice is always dead
Suicide or genocide
Inside the killers head.

I'm tired of the blame game
Admission of guilt
I killed all the love
On which this was built
It was never down to fate
In a world so full of hate
It was greed served on a plate
That produced the empire state

When we build it will they come
Here on earth we need the sun
Can't you see that we're all one
All connected everyone

Foolish Pride.

Gratitudes and platitudes I need a change of attitude.
I'm sorry that I lied, you couldn't stand the truth.
You said you wanted more from me,
I gave you all I could.
I didn't plan it this way
Now you're gone for good.

Are we too broke to fix, jokes are wearing thin.
Use the same old tricks, can a loser win,
Can't adjust my settings, you said it was a sin.
Found a better way, I'm searching within.

Choking on my tears, facing all my fears,
Can I bring you comfort after all these years.
You shrank away from life, wallowed in the strife,
I have to try again; I want you in my life.
Love is not emotion; Love is not a crime,
Love will save us all but we're running out of time.

After all these years, my heart beats faster.
Every time you're gone, my heart beats faster.
When I see your face, my heart beats faster.
After all the tears, my heart beats faster.

Was it foolish pride?
That made me run and hide.
Deep inside of me,
My heartbreak must break free.

Upward Spiral

Dreamt of drinking from your cup,
I got confused which way is up.
I wore the smile to hide my tears,
bravado covered all my fears.
I didn't care where I was thrown,
if someone's there I'm not alone.
Slept inside your septic tank,
it's hard to say how low I sank.
Couldn't bare to wear a frown,
I spiraled up instead of down.

I can't live with this decision,
I can't do the long division.
Cleansed myself of all the hate,
I'm standing at the open gate.
Made a choice not left for fate,
I'm counting on myself.
I bathe inside the golden glow,
it's gonna show me where to go.
So warm inside the undertow,
it's deeper than the ocean's flow.
We're gonna reap what we will sow,
I'm gonna live in love town.
And no ones gonna bring me down,
In love town.

The Zone

I know you thought you got me
and you tried to change my tone,
Got lost in an emotion that seed should not have grown.
It hurts now that you left me but I'm better off alone,
I was lost within your crisis now I got one of my own.

A life of service has no use if broken from the start.
We held together for too long it tore us both apart.
My words still give offence,
my demeanor too intense,
The sad refrain inside my brain,
was sitting on the fence.
I sang this song before I think,
the words they made me tense.
I'm singing now,
I don't know how,
it really makes no sense.

So low but not alone, confronting all my fears.
I'll make a stance, learn to dance, wipe away the tears.
My inner child is running wild, to fill my empty soul.
No more the bitter actor, creation is my goal.

I wonder at the wonders, I'm getting in the zone.
I wonder at the wonders, I'm getting in the zone.

Allegiance

I'm at the checkout strip or chip
Buy a bag and take a trip
Feed the homeless house the feeder
Greedy killer guilty breeder

Should I keep this appointment? The ointment is stinging
The words in my head are constantly spinning
This is my table, what are you bringing?
Is this real life? Then why am I clinging?

Don't be alarmed. What is that ringing?
Is that a siren, why is she singing?

Burn the flagging symbol crash
Smashed and grabbed by petty cash
You bought the lemon with a pledge
Allegiance to the razors edge.

Consumer fears and shifting gears
In a world of shattered schemes
Never trust the well-dressed charlatans
In this market of extremes
They're selling war and glory boys
Will you buy their vicious lie?
A line drawn in the shifting sands
Where poor boys fight and die.

My Atoms

I climbed the spiral staircase
Deep inside my mind
I saw the light so clearly
From all of humankind
Your sadness overwhelms me
I feel it, so it's real
I cannot fix it for you
You've gotta learn to deal

I tried to offer comfort
You said you needed more
You showed me all your sorrow
You told me I was poor
No more the bright tomorrow
Just darkness at my door
Your bittersweet rendition
Will haunt me evermore
Do I have to be a witness?
Detached from this hell
I never saw you stumble
And now I know you fell
You can't control another
So I will call you brother
Love will keep me strong
This earth will be my mother

My Jail has never had bars
My atoms they came from the stars
My Jail has never had bars
My atoms they came from the stars

Clipped Wings

Arrogance will eat you, stop living in the past.
Righteous indignation, nailed you to the mast.
Too damned stiff to bend, refused to try and blend,
You think it's just a trend, are you the bitter end?

The best of times the worst of times, cheers then Mr Dickens.
I rode the bomb in Stangelove, yeah, it's still Slim Pickens.
The Sellers name was Peter, Kato's bomb was ticking.
Erased the fear so Lynch me, shite tastes just like chicken.

This ain't a revelation, there is no revolution,
You are your own solution, your own authority.
Try going with the flow, hold onto letting go.
This culture is a vulture and you don't want to know.
Can you afford the madness of this insanity?
Your stupid game of war is peace, is alien to me.

Devise a better method, actor take a bow.
Be the Chaplin Charlie, Brando save me now.
Devito booked the taxi, DeNiro drove it home.
If Holly would, you'd let her, E.T.'s coming home.

You're tripping and you're slipping
Here's what they've been shipping
A dream of wings for clipping
You're staring at a screen.

Trial

Its too late again and the call is for blood
Well it drives me insane do you hear me?
And why do you call this bloody justice
When you don't even mean it, its just insane.

Invasion of my perfect mind,
Stop my train of thought.
Your killing off the last escape
Forgetting what im taught.
A trial without a jury
A fight without a foe.
Im beaten by the fury
Got nowhere else to go.
A rage an age engage my brain
Take me back to the start again.

Corrosion of my mental state,
Well it's a dying shame.
I have no choice before me,
Got no one left to blame.
Left without an option,
Left without a chance.
Breakdown my connection
And put me in a trance.
A rage an age engage my brain
Take me back to the start again.

You call this some sort of show trial, it's a joke.
Some sort of sick humour.
You just decide, okay this guy we think hes done wrong,
It doesn't matter if he has or he hasn't.
You put people away for years, because you want to,
You want to put em away,
Well it drives me insane for gods sake.
You call this bloody justice, i don't think so.
Its one rule for you.
Its another rule for me.

War Zone (come home)

In a war zone burning breakfast,
a solid state of numbed out mind.
Eating soap stars in vast numbers,
a sense of purpose so hard to find.
A to Zed of the acid zone in a nation of escape.
You see the world through TV's eyes,
We're regressing to the ape.

Burnt out shell of human suffering,
Can't explain the need for war.
Just a worn out gut reaction,
A dirty band-aid on an open sore.

Don't forget to be forgiven,
Understand my life of crime.
You take the chances you've been given
And pass the buck right down the line.
I've been to heaven, man made hell,
I've seen the angel burning bright,
I saw the point where mankind fell,
Can't do wrong for doing right.

Heard the voices on the radio,
Active circuits are in my head.
Trip the light fantastic vision,
Freeze frame and fade to red.
A people's army is killing people,
A dirty band-aid on an open sore.
Stand in line for ethnic cleansing,
Gonna kill kill kill the poor.

How many times can we make the same mistakes?
There's a war going on just outside my door,
And nobody knows what its there for.

Own This

My head was stuffed with nonsense it almost broke my mind.
Tired of your excuses on and on you grind.
I'm not this rising tide and anguish has no pride,
Fixing broken wings and burning up inside.
I sit alone in crowds, chemicals and clouds,
Blinded by the noises deafened by the voices.
I'm driven by compassion that you don't understand,
My energy is endless I'm gonna make a stand.

Programmed my mind and washed my own brain,
I'm circling the drain, again and again.
I've been to your mountain I drank from the fountain,
The fourth wall is broken, the prophet has spoken.
I drank from the source, I built a new road.
The dark horse I ride on deciphered the code.
You're calling me crazy but up I will rise,
Nothing can stop me from reaching the prize.

Not another Sparta, not another Rome.
No more repetition we are coming home.
Home from your war your famine and hate.
Sick of your greed not taking the bait.
Charged up and ready, steady my aim.
Careful not care less the name of my game.
Repealing with passion your dog eat dog rules,
I've said it before, I wont follow fools.

Oppression an obsession
Ignoring your call.
Regression is your weapon
You can't own it all.

Peace Is The Path.

I know that I'm the victim or the victor in your game.
To pit myself against myself time and time again.
This game of life is really just stupid repetition.
As soon as you are able you're in the competition.
To the victor the spoils, is spoiling for war.
It's me versus me that is keeping me poor.
But poverty's not about who has the money.
The system is rigged and I don't find it funny.

I feel that I know and I know that I feel.
Surrounded by chaos, I'm keeping it real.
Don't believe in your guilt or think it's a sin.
I will rise up and I'm searching within.
I challenge myself, that's how I improve.
I know I am ready, to make my next move.
Winning is easy, when you open your eyes.
First do no harm and you still get the prize.

A will to survive, willing to pray
I am desire and I wont go away
You know you mean the world to me
Peace is the path to sweet victory.
A Prisoner of war, I'm not M.I.A.
I am here still and I won't run away
When you're ready, come running to me
Peace is the path to sweet victory.

The Strangers Voice.

The range of my emotions blur,
I make no sense at all.
I hurt myself to help you
I'm heading for a fall.
You say you want my truth again,
You wanted me to try.
The thought police protected you
So you could live that lie.

There's no escape you tell me
You're standing loud and proud.
Committed to the party line
You're playing to the crowd.
I thought you would betray me
Yet love can make you blind.
I could not stop that nagging doubt,
From running through my mind.

I'm not your Big Brother.
I'm not your saving grace.
I see you as the stranger
A voice without a face.
You're lost within this matrix
The dreams are all too real.
The voice is loud within me
It tells me how to feel.
Now the trial is over
I can feel the rising pain.
I lost my sight, this can't be right,
Are you still inside my brain?
Lost and found, sense and sound.
Lost and found, sense and Sound.

Trust Fall.

On love and loss, I've lost it
Worth every precious drop
And I feel the cold of winter's hand
Yet summer will not stop
I'll spring back up to love you
I'm ready for the fall
Stand proud of my survival
And I'm waiting for the call.

The prisoner of my own desire
Ignite the fire that takes me higher
For all my human life requires
One more drop of bliss
I crave your kiss on this precipice
To hold you close once more
We had it all and gambled it
To fill, to fail, to fall

Is there any point to all this nonsense?
Is this drama really necessary?
From the ridiculous to the sublime
Trap the past remembering
One step out of time
I promise to you this fantasy
Dreaming is not a crime
Locked within this fortress projected by my mind.

Unlock your heart you're holding the key
Unlock your heart and give it to me.
Trust Fall, it's a trust fall...

This Abundant World.

I used to think the world would sink,
beneath the tide of change.
Now I see that love is life, I need to re arrange.
My toxic thoughts, were drowning me,
I lost my open mind; I doubted love so foolishly,
How can this be mankind?

How'd we get to this position? Life is not a competition,
Loving life must be our mission, Help me turn this tide.
I tried with all my might, to make the wrong the right
Went down without a fight and left the pain behind.

I want to feel the love of life,
Washing over me.
Like the mighty ocean,
Like the shining sea.
We need to stop and think
There is no planet B.
I have this dream of love
That's where I want to be.
This abundant world
Still belongs to me.

Human Racing?

I've watched you from afar
Up close I see your fear
You wished upon a star
To take you outta here
The mother ship collided
With all that you held dear
Time to face this problem
Change or disappear

Your race was not for space
Your face was out of place
Don't sink without a trace
You're in a state of grace
It's boiling down to this
This place you'll surely miss
I know you didn't plan it
But you're on the precipice

Have you tried just being
Are you tired of seeing
Things go wrong
When you don't do right
Do you hide real history?
Call it a mystery
Or conspire the truth
And continue to fight

The laws of attraction
Are used as distraction
The compass is spinning
Is west still the best?
I see the dividers
A symbol so basic
Try angle controller
Your eye is a test

Racing, why are you racing.
Racing, where are you now.

Middle

I've peeled another layer off
I felt the sting of truth
I felt that savage beauty
Remembered from my youth
A careless giddy feeling
It welled up deep inside
I let go of perception
And i swam against the tide.

You're too quick off the blocks
You'll end up kicking rocks
The school of harder knocks
They'll put you in a box
Your fire has made you blind
It's clouding up your mind
The cruel cannot be kind
And now you're in a bind.

The dream it lingers on
In sleep we dare to dream
In life you couldn't cope
Emotions too extreme
The hope within the heartache
Put you in the dark
The light is in your eyes
The fires about to spark
Does free will get you by
You love the living lie
The real world makes you cry
Now you're not prepared to try
You're living in a cave
Emerge and you will see
The home of the slave
And the land of the fee.

Let's just start again
We need that middle way
The kindness in your heart

Will turn this night to day
Love will heal your harm
The system brings you down
Find the middle way
And turn the whole world around

Where Are You Now?

With the skill of the sculptor
He shaped himself
With the mind of a mad man
He fooled himself
With the hands of sad man
He ruled himself
Now he sits all alone in his tower.

With the passion of an artist
He painted all the pain
His eyes were full of tears
His blindness was insane
With the tools of his trade
He built this charade
And the sadness took over,
took over his brain.

With the heart of a poet
Words cut right through
He looked for a meaning
His passion grew
He searched deep inside
His quest was true
He dreamt of creation.
A better world he knew.

Won't wait until tomorrow
He can't ignore the sorrow
He has to lead not follow
He thinks he will be free.

Praying For The Prayerless.

I will have no imitations, growing tired of those frustrations.
Not dealing with your limitations, I'm real and I am strong.
When all around is expectation, I am here with no fixed nation.
In a world of fascination, that's where I belong.

I'm gonna bring a brighter day, there has to be a better way,
Life should not be shades of grey, stop getting in your way.
Raise your head and raise your voice, rise up now
You have the choice.
Let spirit fly and touch the sky, live your life today.

A few are souls in conflict, I know that can't be right.
They're stuck on repetition and I'm choosing not to fight.
Their way is not the future, for they have lost their sight.
They'll disappear, we don't see fear, we're living in the light.

Its time to dream again,
Lift your hearts and dream again.
Some will call us careless,
We're living in the dream
Praying for the prayerless.

Madmen On Horses.

The cart before the horse
Is full of last years trash
I tried to buy your time
I didn't have the cash
Sleeping in the gutter
A nasty looking rash
The cats still got the cream
And I really gotta dash.

I can't see the downside
I'm still looking up
Gone are the days
I drank from that cup
Make my own choices
Start from within
Lead with the goodness
I know there's no sin.

There has to be a reason
There has to be a rhyme
Cos I won't let you in
And we're running out of time
You really think you're living
We really aren't forgiving
The downsides going up
Turning love into a crime.

Smash The Cage.

The race I was running had got rather cunning,
It twisted my mind infecting my brain.
You plied me with sweetness at first it was stunning,
My ranting subsided, you smiled at my pain.

My flight was curtailed by clipping my wings,
I couldn't feel freedom when so full of rage.
Tempted I emptied my mind of all things.
You saw that within me from inside your cage.

Deep raved I am thriving, not just surviving,
I'm driving back home with love in my heart.
For years I'd been hiding, accused of conniving,
I'm taking the wheel and playing my part.

The mask that I wore restricted my breathing,
I was seething inside and that just wasn't smart,
I stand here before you naked and smiling,
Living my truth through music and art.

Smash the cage, Turn the page, Stop the rage,
I'm making the break, To re-start my heart.

Thorns

I'm joining the resistance
I won't go the distance.
I questioned my existence
And sowed the seeds of doubt.
Do I give the impression?
That I suffer from depression.
It's just another session
Well, I'm English don't you know?

A thorn amongst the roses
A legacy to stand on.
I ain't got nuffin' left
That I can put me 'and on.
A thorn amongst the roses
I rose to shed the crown.
Thorns are in me headspace
There's blood upon my gown.

 I'm giving in, I'm giving out
You must be deaf, I gotta shout.
I'm giving up, I'm giving way
Nothing left, to do but pray.

Try To Understand

I was never really scared and that's probably why I'm scarred
From your club I am barred and I took it kinda hard
But nothing is sacred if nothing is real
I'm seeking the truth and I'm trying to heal

I will try to understand
I don't know where I will land

This wound is bleeding still
Your guilt it comforts nil
You say that you feel nothing
As you take another pill
Is it Damage limitation?
Are you Jesus imitation?
Are you powered by creation?
Is this victim registration?

I will try to understand
I don't know where I will land

The kneejerk collective
Is oh, so effective
It's turning the tide
There's nowhere to hide.
You're pressed into service
A stationary ride
The palace of malice
Is swollen with pride.

I know I know nothing but something is wrong
I bleed what I read while I'm singing this song
All of your dreams are written as lies
Your fear manifested is not a surprise.

I will try to understand
I don't know where I will land

Truly Sorry?

Well here it is in essence, an unapology.
You really should remember how English I can be.
I'm sorry that its over, sun setting on the greed,
I never wanted ugliness, who sowed that little seed?

A promise that was never kept, was never meant to lie,
You said it was free enterprise; lets give it all a try.
It sounded oh so innocent; we mostly wished it well,
Beneath the veil, what we set sail, has landed us in hell.

Now as the sun is setting, we cling to all the gifts,
The things we have collected, between the little rifts.
The shifting sands are on us, our time is almost done,
We should not cry, lets celebrate, the setting of the sun.

Oh yes, we saw this coming; the end was close at hand,
I never thought we loved it, heads buried in the sand.
We tried to rein it in and I'm sure we'll try again,
The greedy one's are steering, was it always in the plan?

I am sorry that its over and I had my share of fun,
But the dream became a nightmare by carrying a gun.
You can't force feed me hunger, or sell me poverty,
I am a human being and I'm choosing to be free.

The Mighty Oak

The war on truth continues to grow its terror tree,
The systemized are stigmatized for trying to be free.
The uninformed think the uniformed will really let them be.
Blinded by their lack of trust and choosing not to see.
I want to quote the wisdom but I'm accused of sin.
Isolated from the pain your sickness is within.
Reminders of the flags you waved.
Bandages and shame.
Upwards, onwards straight you marched
We will not play your game.

Disarmed by smiling children, their innocence you stole.
Standing up for justice, you lied about your role.
If you're the law and lawyer, then you're judge and jury too.
There's truth and then there's untruth, It's really down to you.
Did you fall, did you falter, did you really ask why?
Were you certain, were you righteous, did you fall from on high?
Did you really think this through, were there no seeds of doubt?
You're a monster, you're a god now and I'll call you out.

When I saw through the smoke screen that truth it was fake,
And the liars were lawyers just cutting up the cake,
I went to that party it was more like a wake,
If Justice is just us are we all on the take?

Of the many masks I chose to wear
The one that hides the pain.
Has come to me in dreamtime
And swirls around my brain.
Embrace that contradiction
Defend that bigotry.
The mighty oak is burning bright
For all who want to see.

Compulsive deception the shell game explodes.
My journey to freedom is not on your roads.
Rebuilding from kindness from more not from less.
We follow compassion not your distress.

We see that a border marks your terror tree.
Your limited living will never be free.
Exposing the posers and we will not hide.
Our tribe is the future and we don't divide.

Nigel R Mitchell. A Biography.

As a small child living in the UK during the late 1950's and early 1960's I felt boxed in, like I was being conditioned to accept my place in a class divided world. That was when I started to dream and they were big dreams, vivid dreams. I was yearning for freedom, freedom from limitations, from division, from everything I was being taught. I did not enjoy school; I did well enough there but soon got bored. I skipped most of school after I was 11 years old and pursued the life of a jockey. Riding racehorses gave me a thrill. I rode as a professional Steeplechase Jockey and rode a few winners. That was a blast but had too many limitations for my dreams. I decided to explore my dreams. I pursued a life of music, art and literature. It was a struggle to support myself but I had all the time in the world. I read, wrote, traveled, talked, painted and made music. I got inspired by politics and punk rock in the late 70's and enjoyed the rush of rebellion. I became aware of the system and saw it's controls on my lifestyle and tried to shake the chains off. I backpacked around the world for a year in 1986 and threw away the blinders forever. I unplugged myself from the system and embraced life. My writings and my life are my art, I started a band and called it tunnelmen, it evolved and became tunnelmental, I moved to Los Angeles. I feel it is up to the artist to advance perception. I push harder than the destroyers of beauty. Love and peace are my weapons; say unity.

http://tunnelmental.com/t.e.a./index.html
https://www.facebook.com/nigel.r.mitchell

www.ingramcontent.com/pod-product-compliance
Lightning Source LLC
Chambersburg PA
CBHW071201090426
42736CB00012B/2408